It Goes to the Doer (s)
x
Unemployed Owner

*Simple idea's for the Grind to get
away x stay away from the 9 to 5*

It Goes to the Doer (s)
x
Unemployed Owner

By: Armand Cook

In the beginning of all that
were born with a born in
harmony. We were natural
doers-
We didn't talk ourselves out
of being great x achieving-
doing all that desired x
delight in doing, being.
Never allowing one to get in
our heads.
We prospered!
We Spoke- even though we
we mess up.
We walked- even though we
would fall.
We persisted in the face of
the unknown.

We were triumphant time and
time and time again in a
multitude of things.
Yet as some x most got older
they forgot the basic
principles of doing.
Forgotten or taken out by
life- for the reasons of fearing
of making a mistake.
What others will think- allow
that to stop you.
Wanting to please people that
have their own life yet state
that you should live this or
that way.
Yet this is the time of going
boldly into the unknown.
Being x creating- doing that
which you desire.
While honoring the life x
rights of all.

It all falls on you to do that
things that you want to do.
Yes it is simple yet we will in
a world were most make
excuses for why they cannot-
do not be that person or stop
being that person.
That [thing] that is inside of
you- it is up to you to bring it
to fruition.

It Goes To The Doer (s)
It is a lifestyle x mentality- a
mindset.
In all facets of one's life.
[Big x Small] and all in
between.
It reminds me of August 21,
2017.

This is an instance between
two people that did not know
one another nor did they ever
meet each other and when
faced with the same situation-
did the results vary.
This August 21, 2017- it was
stated that they was going to
be a solar eclipse. I desired to
see it- I said to myself that I
wouldn't view it with of bare
eyes and truly wasn't aware
that there were special
glasses. So I said within my
inner world. I will just use
three or four pair of my
sunglasses.
I did just that- I just as gazed
highly comfortably at the
solar eclipse.

Later- I had a conversation with someone that I know- stating that I view the eclipse and inquiring on if they had view the natural occurrence x phenomena.

They stated to me that they did not have they "special" glasses. I replied that which I did.

They said "That's interesting" because another person they know were going to do that same thing yet the people around him laughed and stated that it wouldn't work.

This instance is how one did and one did not.

The one that did.
-Did not announce, just did.

-Was able to view that which
they desired by using
ingenuity.
-Built another building block
of "doing" within oneself.

Conversely-
the one that did not.
-Peer pressured into not do
that which they desired.
-Did not fulfill themselves.
-Did not view that which they
desired.

In all manners of life-
It Goes To The Doer (s).

One can plan
Create a spreadsheet
Visualize
Listen to podcast
View videos
Yet without *doing* nothing
will come.
It Goes to the Doer (s)

Preface

It is said that:
"From 2010 to 2015, an additional 2.4 millionaires were minted. This comes to a rate of about 1,700 millionaires being made each day, and it is estimated that there will be another 3.1 millionaires created by 2020.
#Facts

You can be one of them- yet don't let millions be the end goal.

#ItGoesToTheDoer
#ItGoesToTheDoers
#UnemployedOwner
#UnemployedOwners

Today is today- Life is life.
What are you going to do
today x with your life.
Everyday you write your
script.
Even if your life is great-
how are you going to make it
better.
Yes be happy x content- be
grateful.
Yet always progressing, in all
facets.
As you accomplish- allowing
you pallet desire better
flavors x more from life.
In all your gaining x doing-
remember to give back.
No you do not have to do so
yet it would be conducive to
humanity as a whole.
-ArmandCook

Acknowledgments

To life- my friend x the
greatest gift that I have ever
known.
You have been with me from
my conception and will be
there with me in the end.
My friend- it is exciting to
know that as the moments
ever flow, to you x I, this is
only the beginning!
I appreciate you exceedingly
so- gratitude for allowing me
to dwell in this realm.
To God- my friend, gratitude
to you for the gift above and
all that you have freely

Introduction
For all those that want more
Look no further
How Come?
For all that you need you
already have
It is Within
Some may think that it is
fluff
Alright fine!
All of you that do-
Leave.
Yes- Simply leave.
Yet
All those that believe and
want more
Let's Imagine
Let's Believe
Let's Build
Allowing them that do not- to
somewhat watch while

keeping our privacy.
Unemployed Owner™
It is but a belief
Combined with Lifestyle-
A Belief that all is possible
While Creating a Lifestyle
that allows one to do as they
please-
That is while respecting the
lives and rights of Humanity.
A belief that the thing that
you have within your mind
and being-
That it can be brought to
fruition!
A Lifestyle
That allows one to yes- enjoy
the pleasures of this life-
Indeed
Yet!

To also Give Back
That is in which ever form
one sees fit.
We are Uncommon
We are Unique
Yet
We Are All Connected.
Belief x Lifestyle
That is who we are and what
we do.
So from Me to You
Be You
Truly
Lift Others Up
Eat Well
Laugh Often
While Yes Many Other Great
Things
Yet Most Us All!
Breaking The Status Quo
Break The Plateau
Thank You.

Mediation is great.
Prayer is great
Yet the best thing is taking
Action, Action, Action!

Don'f forget- you can
-Start late
—Start over
-Be unsure
-Look different
act different
try x fail
and still succeed.

Big things usually have small
beginnings.

When I began my journey, I
hardly had an idea on where
to start. Yet the memory
popped within my my of
2009 summer when I father
had me incorporate some
businesses for him. A way of
him teaching me by practice
x doing.
I am thankful x appreciative
of him doing that.
Yet it was years later when I
decided to create my own and
a lot had slipped my mind.
Yet in this age of the internet-
I placed it in the google
search bar- thank God for
google (also that Google did
not sell itself all those years
ago.)

Though I suppose any search
bar x avenue is sufficient-
yet then I ran into a universe
of information, options and
opinions- websites and blogs
stating a number of things.

I also noticed that a number
of things- the internet itself
had changed tremendously!
Yet in the best of ways- it
was more simple, "easier",
straight forward, more cost
effective and how to make it
legal.

In this age that we live in- it
will go in the "books" as the
start of the greatest time to be
alive. If you are born in land
that is free.

This book as create to
simplify the process of
creating a business, gaining x
earning money.
That way you can enjoy the
facets of life while giving
back if you so choose to do
so.

Here are various businesses x
a simplified blueprint

These are stepping stone to
something more grand
To earn and fortune and gain
a greater fortune and repeat.

Yet lastly- You can have all
the money x knowledge in
the world yet if you do not
have health- neither taste as
good.

Let's get started!

Photography [1]

Go to a secondhand store x find a working camera and equipment
(If it was good enough for photos year ago it's still good now- it produces the same photo that looked great just a few years prior.)
-$300

Build a portfolio x refine your skills

Build a website at Godaddy.com
-$6.99 to $29.99

Advertise to restaurants, schools, nursing homes- etc

Charge $30 per photo session

Do that at least 10 times a week
+$300 per week

Profit: $15,570 per year

Domain Flipping

Obtain yourself a
godaddy.com account or any
other domain purchasing
service provider.

Brainstorm various domain
names and or view domains
that are being sold to get an
idea.

Buy a few to 10 domains
-$100 plus tax

Sell each of them for
+$50 to +$100
Though some domain names
can go for so much more

Do that each week
+500 to $1000 per week
Profit: $20,800 to $46,800
per year

Custom Snapback Range

Design yourself a logo x
brand name

Find a suitable bulk
manufacturer off alibaba.com

Order a range of snapbacks
with brand name and logo
-$800 for 200 hats

Sell 20 snapbacks per day at
$15 each
+$300 per day

Profit: $80,300 per year

For those that say "I don't
have time for a side hustle"

168 hour in a week

50 at work= 118 left

7 at the gym= 111 left

56 for sleep= 55 left

55 free hours a week?

Stop finding excuses!

Study the average second hand selling price of a certain model of car in your area

Monitor Facebook buy x sell pages for cars of that model needing to be sold as soon as possible

Offer $350 below market average, cash in hand

Clean x wax car and take professional photos
-$20

Pay for a classified ad on eBay or craigslist
-$30

Sell for $200 above above market average

Profit: $500 per car or $78,000 per year (3 car per week)

Personal Trainer

Find a local gym
Pay a small fee to train
clients using their facilities
-$50 per week

Charge $75 per hour for a
training session

Train 5 clients per day
+$375 day

Profit: $94,900 per year

<u>Catering Company [1]</u>

Identify popular tourist
attractions within driving
distance of you area

Buy a second hand van
-$15,000

Advertise on trip advisor and
Airbnb as a sightseeing tour

Take 15 people per trip
Charging $50 per person
+750 per trip

Pay fuel and vehicle
maintenance cost
-$500 per week

Operate 5 trips per week (1 a
day)
50 weeks per year

<u>Profit: $154,000 year 1 and
$169,000 every year after</u>

Catering [2]

Buy your own catering
equipment (portable tables,
crockery, cutlery etc.)
-$2,000

Buy ingredients and find a
fired who can cook
-$20 per guest

Cater for events of 20 - 40
people
+$60 per guest

Profit: $1,600 per event

Hair Dresser

Lease a building x space in a
busy area
-$1,000 per month

Buy hairdressing equipment
(clippers, electric supples,
hair products- etc.)
-$2,000

Charge $25 a haircut

3 Hair and hour, 8 hours a
day $600 per day

Profit: 156,000 per year

<u>Copywriter</u>

Sign up of freelancer.com or another freelancing site.

Build your customer base as you write good quality content for blogs or websites

Charge $20 an hour for your services

<u>Work 6 hours per day +120</u>

Don't take a job-
Create one
Don't borrow money-
Lend it
Don't see a problem-
See a solution

If you don't build your dream, someone will hire you to build theirs.

Start *saving x investing money*
Jump on a low budget opportunity
Work your way up from there

Comfort does not make people great!

Dog Walking

Advertise online on gumtree
or craigslist.
Walks for $6 per half hour

Find regular clients and learn
to to 5 dogs at once $30 per
walk

8 walks per day
5 days a week
$210 per day

Profit: $62,000 per year

After School Sports

Choose a sport and buy a
bunch of equipment-
(Soccer Balls, Cones- etc.)
-$300

Advertise to students at local
schools

Charge $20 per students for a
2 hour for after school sports
training session

Run 1 class per day with 20
students per class
+$400 per day

Profit: $146,000 per year

App Developer

Think of a creative idea for a mobile game

Use a site such as upward.com to get year game designed
-$2,000

Market your app to a particular niche on Facebook x Instagram
-$50 per week

Ad revenue pays $6 1,000 ad views.
30k users each viewing 4 ads per day
$720 per day

Profit: $259,480 per year

It's crazy have
people think 2-5
years even 5-12
year in business in
a long time to
become financially
wealthy
Yet do not think
that 40 year at a job
is a long to to stay
broke.

<u>Selling Phone Case</u>

Focus on a particular niche
(Phone case for dog x cat
lovers)

Buy phone case in bulk from
site such as alibaba.com -$0.5
per case

Pay to advertise phone cases
on big Facebook x Instagram
pages in chosen niche
-$50 per week

Sell Cases on Amazon or E
bay
35 cases per day at $8 each
+$280 per day

<u>Profit: $93,212 per year</u>

Create A Cookbook

Compile a list of your
families favorite recipes

Use a site such as blurb.com
to get the book printed
-$5 per book

Sell 8 books per day at $30
per book
+$240 per day

Profit: $72,800 per year

Customised T-Shirts

Create a cool design or
slogan for a T-Shirt

Get the design printed from
an online print-on-demand
service
-$100 for 50 shirts

Sell 10 shirts per day at +$20
per shirt

Profit: $65,520 per year

Dropshipping

Find a niche
(Yoga Mats)

Buy mats from suppliers in
China on sites such as
aliexpress.com
-$2 per mat

Market on Amazon.com
Ship directly from suppliers
when purchase is made

Sell 10 mats per may at +$15
per mat

<u>Profit: $47,320 per year</u>

Extra Income Ideas

1.) List a room in your house
2.) Create an e-commerce store
3.) virtual assistant
4.) Get paid using your car- deliver food for restaurants
5.) Edit videos
6.) Affilate marketing
7.) Teach english and math
8.) Start a blog
9.) Check you coins to see if they are valuable.
10.) Sell your pictures
11.) Publish an ebook
12.) Personal branding
13.) Freelancing (Skill)
14.) Flipping Items on eBay

Save to invest x earn.
Be decisive.
Take risk.
Watch out for who you spend
your time with.
Watch your thought and
actions.
Invest in yourself.
Focus on the numbers x
percentage.
Go for 10 to 100 times the
amount.

Fixing iPhone Screens

Practice replacing screens on broken decides to master the art

Hand out flyers and put up posters to market your services locally

Buy iPhone screens in bulk from China
-$130 for 10 screens

Fix 6 screens per day at $55 each
+$330 per day

Profit: $91,980 per year

Music Teacher

Advertise on noticeboard at local school school or even ask to go in and talk to classes

Charge $30 per student for a 1 hour lesson

Teach 4 students per class
Take 3 classes per day
+$360 per day

Profit: $129,600 per year

Window Cleaning

Buy necessary equipment
[Ladders, water fed pole,
brushes, water purifier etc.
-$1,000

Create a website, logo, and
brand.
Market online via social
media.

Pay for fuel and
transportation cost
-$200 per week

Charge $32 per hour- work 8
hours per day, 5 days a week
+1,280 per week

<u>Profit: $56,160 per year</u>

Selling Throw Pillows

Focus on a niche
Typical target audience is
female homeowners
Aged 30-55

Buy throw pillows in bulk off
sites such as alibaba.com
-$2 per pillow

Advertise on Facebook x
Instagram focusing on your
niche

Sell 20 pillows per day at $12
per pillow
+$240 per day

Profit: $73,000 per year

Make more moves and less announcements.

Smart people think.

Brave people talk.

Great people act.

Airbnb Host

Great if you have a spare
bedroom or secondary suite

Take nice pictures of the
room and create and Airbnb
listing

Provide your guests with a
key on arrival and give them
tips on what to see x do in the
area

Rent out 2 rooms for 300
nights per year at +$60 per
night
(Area Dependent)

Profit: $36,000 per year

48

<u>Social Media Marketing Agency</u>

Choose a niche-
Real estate, accounting, e-commerce, etc.

Grow a social media page in said niche.
-$300 per month per page

Reach out to businesses in chosen niche.
Offer to grow their social media presence.
Show your page as an example.
30 customers at $600 per month
+$18,000 per month

Profit: $108,000 per year

Graphics Design

Sign up as a freelancer on sites such as freelancer.com x upwork.com

Create a website x Instagram page with all your work to date.

Forward traffic from your website x Instagram page to your freelancing account

Complete 2 projects per day at $150 per project +$300 per day

Profit: $109,500 per year

Wake up early.

Work harder than
your did yesterday.
Make time to read
every single day.

Never go than 3
day without
exercise

Be a minimalist
Face your fears
Learn daily
Love the act of
work

Desk Organizers

Buy desk organizers in bulk
from a website such as
alibaba.com
-$2.5 each

Advertise through Facebook
to people who work 9-5 desk
jobs

Contact large companies and
ask to put up ads on
noticeboards

Sell 20 organizers per day at
$10 each
+$200 per day

<u>Profit: $54,750 per year</u>

Bespoke Suits

Get in contact with a tailor in Thailand

Create a website where customers can enter their measurements and choose their desired fabric.

Send measurements to tailor and get the suit made to fit
-$100 per suit

Ship to Europe x USA
-$50 per suit

Sell 10 suits per week at $350 per suit
+$3,500 per week

Profit: $130,000 per year

Wedding Photography [2]

Buy a high quality digital
camera x lenses
-$3,500

Create a website of your best
work and market your
services on social media
-$300 per week

Shoot photos for 2 weddings
per week at $1,200 shoot

Profit: $109,200 per year

<u>Handy Man Business</u>

Buy basic tools x equipment
(hammer, pliers,
screwdrivers- etc)
-$2,000

Advertise your services
locally and online.
Build a brand.

Customers contact you for
maintenance work.
Staining a deck, repairing
fences, installing a screen
door.

Charge yourself out at $30
per hour.
Work 10 hours per day
+$300 per day

<u>Profit: $78,000 per year</u>

Lease old building in vibrant area
-$3,000 per month

Refurbish interior into pub
-$30,000

Sell 1 Drink per minute (average)
Between 7 PM and 1 AM at $10 per drink
+$3,600 per day

Pay for stock and other operating costs
-$1,000 per day

Operate 7 days per week
50 weeks per year

<u>Profit: $845,000 year 1 and $875,000 every year after</u>

Practice and go for that
which is real-
1000% over that
which is fake x a
looks

<u>Youtube Channel</u>

For those who believe they
could provide content that
others would be interested in

Create a series of videos and
upload content regularly to
keep viewers interested

Ad revenue pays $7 per 1,000
ad views.
50k subscribers each viewing
1 video per day
$350 per day

<u>Profit: $127,400 per year</u>

Fix Broken Laptops

Great for if your have skills x
interest in working with
electronics

Buy faulty laptops very cheap
off craigslist or gumtree
-$100 each

Fix 2 Laptops per week

Resell the working laptops on
craigslist or gumtree
+$800 each

Profit: $72,800

Home Tutoring

Choose a subject that you have excellent knowledge in

Put together material that would effectively teach the subject

Market yourself at local schools and online on tutoring websites

Tutor 3 students per day at $60 per 2 hour lesson
+$180 per day

<u>Profit: $46,800 per year</u>

<u>Gym Owner</u>

Rent out a suitable warehouse
building
-$5,000 per month

Purchase an array of weight x
exercise equipment
-$50,000

Build a brand and advertise
extensively

300 members at $50 per
month
+$15,000 per month

<u>Profit: $120,000 per year</u>

Two bank accounts in life
emotional and financial
more are not successful
because of the financial bank
account- they run out of the
emotional bank account

*It's not what happens to you
in life it how you react to that
which happens to you in life.*

Create Your Own Beverage

Spend some time learning to
create.
Plenty of information is
available online.

Start by bottling your first
few batches and giving away
to family x friends.

Sell at local markets or
through online craft beer
communities

Sell 15 crates per week
Each with 24 bottles at $40
per crate +$300 per day

Profit: $31,200 per year

Yoga Instructor

Rent a suitable building
-$5,000 per month

Market yourself locally
Put up notices at nearby
gyms.
Create a website.
Pay for Instagram ads.
Offer free trail sessions.

Charge $10 for a 1 hour yoga
session.
20 people person session.
3 sessions per day.
+$600 per day

<u>Profit: $96,000 per year</u>

Travel Blog

Create a website x social media pages and build up a large, engaged following.

Partner with companies such as Airbnb x booking.com

Earn 35% of the commission for every booking made based on your recommendation

35 bookings per day at $120 per booking average +$367 per day

Profit: $134,137 per year

*A great person and a weak
person has the same fear yet
one of them response to it in
a different x effective way*

Said above and said again now

It is said that:
"From 2010 to 2015, an additional 2.4 millionaires were minted. This comes to a rate of about 1,700 millionaires being made each day, and it is estimated that there will be another 3.1 millionaires created by 2020. #Facts

You can be one of them- yet don't let millions be the end goal.

#ItGoesToTheDoer
#ItGoesToTheDoers
#UnemployedOwner
#UnemployedOwners

The 21/90 rule

It takes 21 days to build a habit and 90 days to build a lifestyle.

—

Twenty minutes of doing something is more valuable than twenty hours of thinking about doing something.

Making it legal

How to get a EIN x LLC

It's quite easy

I opened a few businesses x LLC's and when I went to the bank to open an account the banker asked my if I desired for them to open my future LLC's x Businesses through them- I replied "no- no thank you. It's actually pretty easy fill out said paper work, send to the State, receive it back from the State, fill out the form for the EIN with the IRS- it only takes about 10 minutes and the max time you can spend on the EIN form is 15 minutes or it'll time you out and done!

Go to the bank with at least $50 USD, open a checking x savings account that'll be another $50 and Boom- you are in business legally and ready for payments. (now it is even easier) depending on said State- one is able to fill out the LLC form online, pay with your card and Ba Da Boom Ba Da Bing- LLC! They'll email you a copy if all is filled out correctly or send it through the mail if you prefer that way. Then also place it online that way you can view that one and all the others you create."

They sat- looked and smiled.
How come?
For they know how easy it is-
On x Off topic- I have no
issue with banks, I enjoy
them and are fond of them.
Alright back on- on topic.
They know how easy it is-
yet there and many places
that will charge you $50 to
200+ to do said paperwork.
Something that literally took
them less than 25 minutes.
Also that doesn't include the
cost that it takes to open the
LLC in your State.
For the EIN license form the
IRS is free of charge.

I say this part of the writing
because that was our
dialogue- that is that which
they said to me.
That which I heard with my
own ears!
Yet
Understand that people are
not a charity and they should
be properly compensated for
goods x services render.
Point Blank Period.
This is America!
Yet
Understand why they do this
x are they able to do this-
think about it, do you know
why?

The individuals lack of knowledge in said area, fear and anxiety of the unknown. (Yet know worries for there is a universe full of information.)
That is the only reason they get paid for doing something so simple and that will only take you and them 15 to 30 minutes to finish the entire process.
Yet here is the kicker!
We all don't know… UNTIL WE KNOW!!
Yet we can learn!

Ever learning- if one so
chooses to learn.
So why I am having a one
way conversation with you?
1.) For I have some to say x
share.
2.) You desire to create and
learn how to do something
foreign yet simple for Free x
yourself.
Saying all this to say-
Let's have fun- I always
thought that learning should
be simple and fun
Let's be relaxed
Let's have it so that the
creation x voice within you
can now be placed into a
book x ebook.
Lastly- let me help you.
Let's begin!

Before we get started!

What would be best before you start any thing?

You
You
You
and You.
Faith x Persistence
A decision
Realize the cost of both out comes of the spectrum.
1.) Side is to conform and do the status quo- look one day and see someone your age and or much younger doing exactly that which you were going to do.
The other side of the spectrum-
2.) Do that which you desire x delight in doing while honoring the life and rights of all.
Seeing it through- facing

75

yourself each day,
understanding that it's all on
you.
Know that you will do that
which is legally required to see
said thing come to fruition.
Then seeing it in all it's glory-
yet knowing that even in that
moment it is only the beginning.
Start and make it even better-
ever innovating.
Yet pleased with that which you
have done.

Both have a cost-
Number 2 will cost a certain
amount yet the pay off is
infinitely better than number
one- living a life that you do not
desire x delight in for the rest of
your life.

Lastly understand that there are
moments x phases and at times
each are stepping stones x keys
to thing much greater.

Take hold of the opportunities
of [Now] Live Live Live

People Don't know that
Money is a tool. They don't
want to invest, save nor care
about money [that which
money can do] nor the future.

—Security is not a real thing
nor is money- [It is yet again
it isn't.]
—Though there is a way to
have higher chances of
security or take care of
various things that arise x
could arise.
—It is by the concept x piece
of cotton and flax, that is cut
into a triangle with a
Presidents or

inventors face on it.
—That is back up by a metal
that comes naturally from the
ground.

[Money]
Money is a tool
Money is energy
Money- is the thing that
greases the wheel.
—I once had a conversation
with someone that stated that
money can not buy
happiness.
I laughed- I stated something
along the lines of "Is that so?
Tell me what does."
They stated "Love"
I rebuttal with"What about
those that take their life- don't

they have loved ones- those
that love them ever so
deeply? Yet they still take
their life" (At this point I
stated more yet this is a
sound bite). So we see that it
isn't love that buys happiness.

Happiness is dependent upon
oneself- If one is happy
because they desire x chose
to be happy then all things
can flow x bring joy to their
life.
For who has ever been
annoyed by being able to
feed their family?
Who has been unhappy
giving to the homeless or
paying for their own home?
No one!

There is a order to it all-
My personal order is:
God
Health
Family
Money
Humanity
[Here is another sound bite,
though there is more to it]
—God, for He is my
everything, my supply yet
most importantly my friend.
—Health for it allows my to
provide, protect- etc for
myself x my family.
—Family, for family is
everything.
—Money for the things that
is can do.
It makes it so that one can
explore all the facets of life.

[Our PlayGround Earth x Life-
For Live Is A PlayGround]
—Humanity for I love the
philanthropy x charity- helping
others, it is bliss!
—Having God first, it
balances everything out for me
that is-
Yet has one has to choose
happiness- they must also
choose God- if they desire to
do so.

He brings a grand order to it
all.

Money is a tool x the tool of
this playground we call life.
[Lastly- about those taking
their life- that is highly serious
and if you are thinking x
feeling a certain way get help-
it is okay. Also if you know
someone that is struggling- be
there for them x help them
obtain help.]

It Goes to the Doer x Unemployed Owner

Thursday, December 14, 2018
8:40 PM

© It Goes to the Doer (s)
©Unemployed Owner

This edition published in 2018 by
Armand Cook
It Goes to the Doer (s)™
x
Unemployed Owner™

©Armand Cook

United States of America

The right of Armand Cook to be
identified as the author of this work

ArmandCook.com
PostalMontage.com
ItGoesToTheDoer.com
IGoesToTheDoers.com
x
UnemployedOwner.com

<u>Contents</u>